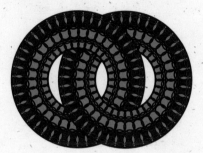

Little
Boy
Blue

Little Boy Blue

A MEMOIR

IN VERSE

Gray Jacobik

CavanKerry ◊ Press LTD.

CavanKerry Press Ltd.
Fort Lee, New Jersey
www.cavankerrypress.org

Library of Congress Cataloging-in-Publication Data

Jacobik, Gray.
Little boy blue : a memoir in verse / Gray Jacobik. -- 1st ed.
p. cm.
ISBN-13: 978-1-933880-22-8 (alk. paper)
ISBN-10: 1-933880-22-8 (alk. paper)
1. Jacobik, Gray--Poetry. I. Title.

PS3560.A249L57 2011
811'.54--dc22

2010017669

Cover photos Gray Jacobik © 2011

Cover and interior design by Gregory Smith

First Edition 2011, Printed in the United States of America

LAUREL BOOKS
CavanKerry◊Press

Little Boy Blue is the eighth title of CavanKerry's Literature of Illness imprint. LaurelBooks are fine collections of poetry and prose that explore the many poignant issues associated with confronting serious physical and/or psychological illness.

CavanKerry is grateful to the Arnold P.Gold Foundation for the Advancement of Humanism in Medicine for joining us in sponsoring this imprint. Offering LaurelBooks as teaching tools to medical schools is the result of shared concerns--humanism, community, and meeting the needs of the underserved. Together with the Gold Foundation, CavanKerry's two outreach efforts, GiftBooks and Presenting Poetry & Prose, bring complimentary books and readings to the medical community at major hospitals across the United States.

CavanKerry Press is grateful for the support it receives from the New Jersey State Council on the Arts.

OTHER BOOKS BY GRAY JACOBIK

Jane's Song, Koinonia, 1976 (chapbook)

Paradise Poems, Omega 3 Press, 1978

Sandpainting, Washington Writers' Publishing House, 1980

The Double Task, University of Massachusetts Press, 1998

The Surface of Last Scattering, Texas Review Press, 1999

Brave Disguises, University of Pittsburgh Press, 2002

Fullest Tide: Poems of Ann Silsbee, CustomWords, 2006
(selected, edited, and introduced by Gray Jacobik)

Contents

Lord, have mercy on my son: for he is
lunatick, and sore vexed: for ofttimes
he falleth into the fire, and oft into the water.

—*Matthew 17:15*

From the beginning I was both necessary
And beside the point, the kid always
The kid, whom you'd overlook completely
Did he not break your heart.

—Joe Bolton, "In Pieces,"
from *The Last Nostalgia*

NOTE

There are three fathers mentioned in the following pages. "Your first father" refers to my son's biological father; "your second father" refers to my second husband, who adopted my son when he was four years old; "your stepfather" refers to my third and present husband—a part of our lives since my son was twelve. There are few names mentioned in the poem itself, and only incidentally: for privacy, these have been changed. Also, one place name is changed.

for Mason, Caden & Jacob

Little
Boy
Blue

Three days passed before you found your
    way to the crook of my arm;
that's why Marilyn Monroe was a part of it.

Two days because you were born jaundiced,
    so they transfused your blood, kept
you in the nursery—that era when any woman

could get lost for the tease she was & the power
    it gave her—when Presidents could,
at the swankiest hotels, order call girls brought up

on service elevators. Roe vs. Wade hadn't
    happened or you'd not have been
born. I did try to find & couldn't, a back-alley

abortionist in the Negro district of Newport News,
    then took thirty pills of quinine
your father's football coach gave him to give me,

leaving me in a coma for three days, pills that
    didn't chase you from my body,
although years later I'd learn the tooth buds that

failed to grow in your mouth were caused by the quinine,
    & who knows, maybe your bipolar disorder,
maybe your ADHD, & back then doctors thought

nothing of keeping a mother from her newborn
      or a newborn from his mother; besides,
the spinal block I'd finally gotten, when I needed

surgery, three hundred stitches to sew up
      a ruptured womb (for the labor was induced
before either of us was ready), meant I was flat out

with lightning pain across my scalp, spasms ruling
      my back, plus the soreness of labor,
delivery, surgery. I woke angry, crying, jealous

of the mother in the next bed over, her son
      born the day you were, white trash
your grandmother had called her, a girl, as I was,

from one of the Eastern Shore's backwater towns.
      Her baby came for twenty minutes as scheduled
eight times a day. The radio between our two beds

said Marilyn Monroe was dead, an apparent suicide.
      August 5th, 1962. Kennedy was President.
I was eighteen. Nobody breastfed babies back then,

especially the poor who aspired to imitate the well-off
      as they still do. You had a cut at the back
of your neck, & all I wanted was to unwrap you,

look at you whole although I was awash with
      the desire, that first time, but often thereafter,
to shove you back up inside me as if you were

an homunculus, a little man & not an infant;
  for there, in the empty doubt
of my body, no one could hurt you. But you

cried & didn't stop crying for six months,
  & the travesties, those injurious acts
that ravel & twist the heart, had just begun.

2

Not quite two years since you sat in your white truck

in my driveway, your two toast-brown dogs
in the seat beside you, eager to go, & you
telling me your girlfriend is a good person,
& you love her, news which gladdens me

though you won't believe that, for how seldom
have you loved anyone? Way back behind
the heavy green dazzle of late September light,
somewhere in the sadness I felt at your leaving,

I knew I'd never see you again, you & the truck
& the dogs & the woman, who is not here
but who's said you cannot ever speak to me
again, for she won some game of her design,

you the prize, me the loser, some struggle she sees
between good, aligned with her, evil, aligned
with me, & you, there, compliant, ready
to go; although I see you are sick with the pain

of it, your face wincing before you harden yourself
once more, your head bowed as if you'd been
sentenced. I hear again, that awkward, tuning-fork
hum of the silence that's always been between us.

Pussy-whipped, your stepfather says of you
as if that might explain what has taken you away
this time. A vagina opening within the dusty-rose
folds, or purple-red folds, or ivory-rose folds

of the vulva, or stretched to the brink of tearing,
or tearing jaggedly, or closed forever, withering
to slime in the casket, or burning to a half ounce
of ash in the crematorium, the vagina, clitoris,

vulva, only a woman's genitals, not a force
of division & yet division begins at this site.
After the moment of crowning comes the head,
the pressed-tight little face, rounded shoulders,

slick bulb of the buttocks, thighs, feet, cord, blood.
But this is a bloodless separation: you are going
into your own life, late, in your forties, to struggle
& suffer as you will, to try, to succeed or fail

to separate yourself again from someone who sees
her survival dependent on yours, & you on hers.
Because distortion is here & betrayal, disbelief
on my part has nothing to do with it. An imperative

as fierce as any we humans know, what belief
can do when it is painstakingly encoded as thought,
what we cannot know or know we do not know—
the fate we make of what we say, not the one born to.

3

Channel surfing I find one of those nanny-knows-best
shows. Nanny takes over & mommy & daddy &

three towheaded brats begin to see slight flickerings
of a possible ordered existence; then the insistent

screams & wide-flung limbs of the boy who's three
remind me of how you'd hurl yourself against any wall

at daycare when I'd try to leave, or in our tiny apartment
whenever you felt frustrated or thwarted—or who

knows why?—neighbors banging on the floor above
or pounding the hall door yelling they'd call the landlord

if I didn't shut that kid up. You'd hurl yourself
as if you intended to shatter your body, then you'd

slide down & pinwheel kick, screaming, flailing,
spinning on your back, your face blood-red,

tear-soaked, gasping for breath that, once caught,
fueled still louder screams. I'd straddle you

with my feet or on all fours doing a kind of war jig
above you to block your head or a leg or hand

from coming down hard on the edge of something.
But not to stop you. I couldn't stop you.

Such fury dazed me, &, later, holding
your spent & hot body, rocking you to sleep,

singing *Hush, Little Baby* or *Tura-Lura-Lural*,
entranced by the scent of your soft hair,

I'd pretend we were a tribe of two, confused
mother & furious child, two who couldn't see

the tragedy or the comedy of it—that our torment
didn't mean anything, anymore than our happiness did.

4

The wake the ferry's engines
churned up widening into
lacework, that plume of white

on a pewter sea, that's what
tempted me. I was riding
a Trailways back to school,

the bus having wound its way
through six flat snow-dusted
corn-stubble counties & now

stood car-bound below deck crossing
the wide mouth of the Chesapeake,
Cape Charles to Old Point Comfort.

Hours before, as your grandmother
stood at the sink & I by the stove
in that weakly framed house

once used by tenant farmers—
now rented to a school nurse
& a printer & their five children—

I told her I was pregnant.
That mouth of hers so often
pinched around a menthol,

fell open to a blank hole &
she sunk down to a kitchen
chair. Then—not a whisper,

not a cry—but slowly & tightly
enunciated, *How could you do
this to us? How could you*

*shame us like this? Have you
no self-respect? No decency?*
I was at the rail thinking

about how to climb onto it
& hurl myself into the wake.
No "right to life" on my mind.

Not yours. Not mine. Only
the need to no longer be.
A passion to obliterate.

The wind shoved my coat
or the ferry jerked—
a sudden forward surge.

I slammed into the rail.
The dream broke & I
went down below deck

& climbed back into
the high dark bus riding
the bay's cold waves.

Twice more in the years ahead,
I came close, but this is the one
I still feel, that shove, that jerk,

it wakes me from sleep
with a start, my guardian
body leaping in front of me.

5

A few months before you left for good, your girlfriend
called & said I had abandoned you seventeen times,
didn't deserve a son. You'd told her this. Seventeen?

Such perceptions are not to be quarreled with, but when
the night won't let my sorrow go, I begin to count:
I forgot you once at Precious Cargo Daycare—the irate

worker, your joy climbing into our car, a fall evening,
the ground wet. And when you were ten, although you'd
spent the spring with me, I sent you back to your
       grandparents.

You were shuffled back & forth after your first father
abandoned us, after I left your second father, & when
the neighborhood became too dangerous; when

my housemates said the kid went or I did, & I didn't.
It is true, mostly, I didn't want you—didn't want to be
a mother. Had I been less ignorant, less restless,

had I had a life before your life became the one I was
supposed to put first, but couldn't; had you not been
the tormented typhoon you were, bed-wetter,

toy-breaker, food-thrower, scrapper, kicker, screamer,
a day & night fury. My doing—the bed I'd made . . .
Not a bed. The front seat of a 1956 Chevrolet sedan,

two-toned green, my grandmother's car, borrowed
one night for a date when your father-to-be came
looking for me in Virginia after he'd hitch-hiked

for sixty-three hours from Fort Bliss, Texas, where
he'd just finished boot camp, at seventeen, having
lied to get in, poor Army-brat kid trying to make his

Colonel Daddy proud of him, & I his only solace,
he mine. It was November & still the crickets sang.
We'd parked where couples always parked in that

town, Chesapeake Avenue, across from the lights
of Norfolk. But all the harm done to you afterwards,
yes, my selfishness as you say. I can't explain the

force in me I couldn't suppress. I wanted more
than I'd ever had, experiences I'd caught hints
of in books. That's putting it simply & it wasn't simple.

O little boy in your orange & blue-striped shirt
& khaki shorts, your blue Keds—I see you shrinking
in my rearview—your brave half-wave, that big-sad

hurt in rubbed-red eyes. You turn & walk off
holding someone's hand. Or I tuck you in & leave
to cross town to a lover's bed, come back by morning,

or not, sometimes not before you'd had breakfast
or gone to school. Although I never left you alone,
I left, alone, & left you behind, & yes, sent you

away to a boarding school, finally, relieved & free,
the only place that would have you without Ritalin
in your bloodstream, the neuron-slowing "speed" that

killed your spirit with its ever-higher dosages needed
to stupefy you—demanded of me or you weren't
allowed in second grade, third, fourth, fifth . . .

But it was me, my fantastic effort to be better, learn more,
be richer, smarter, outshine anyone & everyone
who'd ever said I was to blame for getting pregnant

in the first place. Seventeen. You think it only seventeen . . .

6

I hate the facts as much as you do: our just-another-
        American-story strewn
throughout with the usual mass-produced consumer
        cheapness. All true, the over-
whelming melodramatic tackiness, the *de-crap-itude*,
        including your aunt's
thirty-six day coma, her brain damage that's wrought
        one family tragedy after
another such that your cousin, right now, with no
        sense of remorse, is in
an Orlando prison for selling meth & grand larceny,
        the last of your grandfather's
life savings having gone to pay restitution to his victims.

Divorces, foreclosures, accidents, lawsuits, abortions,
        & seven thousand other
dramatic occasions—poverty's ravishments. And on it
        goes.
        One moves as far away
as possible, holds it at arm's length. Your second father's
        icy heart nearly killed me.
As it turned out, he was gay, & after *aversion hypnosis*
        ("when you desire a man,
you will feel nauseous") failed to work, other *lifestyle
        choices* were called for,
but I'd left by then & taken you & your sister,
        moved to a commune.

He brought all his stupidities into our marriage, & I made
     fancy cakes & puddings
out of them since I was still my mother's daughter,
     living out her dream
to marry into White Southern Aristocracy (instead of the
     Brooklyn-Jewish
hoypoloi she got). Thoroughly sexist, of course, &
     his racism, well, call it
anti-whiteism. He'd rather have been a Black man than
     the white homosexual
he turned out to be, perhaps because the only true
     compassion he'd known
came to him from the men & women who worked
     for his family on that
decaying antebellum estate in Carloville, Alabama, that
     red-clayed, pecan-treed,
fire-ant haven of malignant neglect & ossified traditions.
     Thus his move to the slums
of Baltimore to be near his true folk, & the ex-con drug
     addict who's beaten
him nearly to death repeatedly, gone back to prison
     for it, been forgiven by him
& given him AIDS, & who, of late, bought smack with
     every cent of your &
your sister's inheritance—well, that's accounted for in
     some
     theory of just-recompense
that may or may not relate to an individual life. But what
     does this have to do with you, with me?

He came into your life when you were four & you began
     to stutter. He'd scream at you,

Get it out! Get it out of your goddamn mouth! walking away
      from you whenever
you tried to talk to him, & then I'd scream at him
      for screaming at you, &
that only made matters worse. We lived in post-war
      temporary housing,
still temporary twenty years after the war. You may
      remember the neighborhood—
a school across from us, playground on the corner, where,
      once, on your blue bike
you were hit by a car. I remember the long Western
      vest your second father liked
to wear. It was dyed purple & he'd get high on a few tokes
      & swing the leather fringe
back & forth, rocking in his boots, swishing his long
      brown hair across his face,
blissed-out, grinning. The only time he ever looked free.

He was the third man that year, the year I was twenty-two,
      to propose to me,
& my mother wanted us out of the house, so I married
      him, knowing him only
six weeks. He was a virgin, I was, well, promiscuous.
      Little Boy Blue, sweet,
wild, little child. I see you trying to 8block the door when
      we were leaving on our honey-
moon, November 1966 & we drove to New Orleans.
      I wore a silk-&-lace peignoir
that night, pretending to be a real bride, but the cheap try
      wasn't lost on me.
Still, out of this, we got your good & loving sister.

7

You were a funny kid though, kept us in stitches.
You made up little rituals. Your grandfather
likes to tell of how you'd begin a left-right face,
arm-swinging goose-step march from wherever
you were into the bathroom, crying out *hep-two,*
hep-two. Once there you'd square off, click heels,
center yourself before the toilet, then bark out,
lid up! pants down! underpants down! then *squirt!*
reversing the order of your commands after the act
was done, your aim the usual aim of a four-year-
old. If your aunts & I were still laughing or
struggling not to when you marched back in,
you'd take umbrage & withdraw, for we were
to understand the seriousness of this. How I wish
I could, just once, kneel down before that boy,
as I would then, & apologize for laughing,
take you in my arms, kiss your cheek or forehead,
& hold your little body against mine.
No one was supposed to laugh at you,

                      but, my god, you were funny.

8

The day Picasso dies, April & the cherry trees
are pink as pink chiffon skirts, the sunlight shade-

mottled, grass dandelion-dotted. Whenever I imagine
an afterlife & that old cliché about some saint

stepping up & saying you can have one day back
to live again on Earth, this is the one I choose—

just the three of us—you're eleven, your sister's five.
Your way of telling me you're tired of living

with your grandparents is to say, "I'm not needed
there any more," but today we're on the farm in

Linden, Virginia, the foothills of the Shenandoahs.
Fiery Run is the name of the stream that zigzags

through the front pasture, where the two chestnut
horses, Nosey & Pokey, usually graze, & Fiery

Run is what *we* call the farm—the communards
& I who live in the city & rent this country

place for a year. You & your sister play house
in a tiny unused chicken coop we've swept out

& hosed down. You are content & absorbed,
fixing that little house up & pretending an orderly,

safe life of small domestic tasks. She is her usual
pacific self, bustling to do what you ask of her,

& I spend my day sitting under an apple tree
watching & listening to the two of you, or running

into the house or barn to find some item you
think is needed to make your house more homey.

I love you both so absolutely at that moment
I keep feeling betaken or transfixed, something

on that order—swayed out of time. For that day,
at least, we live in the peaceable kingdom

of fairytales. Once, at midday, you poke your
head through a glassless window & say,

"Mom, you're most like a zebra—calm & flashy."

9

You'd run from driveway
to corner, &, if not retrieved
(kicking, screaming), cross

the street to the playground,
then scamper into the woods
as if summoned or compelled.

Hyperactive was the diagnosis.
What, in the ancient world,
would they have said of you?

Or in Charlotte Bronte's? Spawn
of Dionysus? Imp? Hellion?
And yet such a sweetness

in you too, a tender-heartedness
& sympathy. You were, I think
now, hypersensitive, living

in a culture that had to brutalize
you. I know I had a part in that.
By the time you were five

you'd begun speaking for dogs,
cats, birds, any small creature—
from falsetto to bass you'd

create voices: Bonnie,
our Dalmatian—*Ruff. Ruff.*
We gotta move back to our

old house. Ruff. I gotta dig up
the bone—ruff—I buried
by the big tree. Or for the cat—

I want a G. I. Joe for my birthday
even though I'm a girl. Then,
in your voice—*Mehitabel's*

birthday is tomorrow, not next
week. My birthday is next week.
You'd orchestrate animal

morality plays, voicing conflicts,
fears, desires, the rule each
creature was to abide by, end

with a kiss-&-make-up scene.
How astonishing it was, at times,
just to behold you—*the shapes*

a bright container can contain.
I have a sketch I made of you
at four—down-turned mouth,

eyebrows pinched, the angle you
hold your head—by then you
were sorrowful, wistful, already

Little Boy Blue on speed, running.

10

When you came home again, after a decade
    in California, age forty, your marriage over,

your girlfriend chasing you out with the dogs
    while she sold the house, bedraggled

& frightened after four days & nights
    in your truck crossing the country—

I showed you the room I'd prepared for you
    & you said, *Mom, this is too nice for me.*

A few days later, burrowing in, you hung
    sheets as makeshift walls, drew the blinds,

blackened the skylight, preferring, as always,
    the compact, dark, & cordoned-off,

the tiniest & untidiest of places. Twenty years
    earlier, you'd made your bed in the laundry

room, next to the furnace & water tank.
    When I'd do the wash, I'd find empties

of DeKuyser's Peppermint Schnapps, cheap,
    one hundred proof. Self-medicating

on liquor or dope, as you had since fifteen,
    you now had the will-to-oblivion once mine

& if I tried to stop you, you weren't beyond
        shoving me or taking a swing. Your next

move, when you worked for a plumber,
        was to a rooming house in Leominster,

a triple-decker with rambling additions
        where welfare mothers, their kids, &

a few neglected elderly lived. One January night,
        your cigarette ignited your mattress.

A smoke alarm woke the man across the hall
        who got you out. Fire trucks, sirens,

woke everyone else. When I arrived, driving
        through a blizzard, your smoking mattress

lay on the snow, ice-edged even as it smoldered.
Still smashed, stumbling, weeping & rocking,

 hair singed, arms swinging—you punch-hit
the red flares & revolving lights—

refused to come back home with me.
        I saw it was true—you didn't want to live.

The first time you burrowed, you were nine,
        living in a house I rented with another woman

& two men. You staked out a closet, maybe
        three-by-eight, would sleep nowhere else,

made a cocoon, one thing piled on another.
  So many small spaces I've seen you build

over the years—self-designed Murphy beds,
  collapsible desks, cubbyholes. Your first

website video-clipped the marijuana factory
  you'd created in a closet: silver-lined walls,

full-spectrum around-the-clock lights, automatic
  misting, closed-circuit camera on the plants.

This was the rooming house in Ukiah,
  where cokeheads & dealers lived, where,

through a corner window, lured by your budgie,
  Netanyahu, Western jays & pigeons flew

into your room. You'd trained Net to shower on
  your shoulder & whistle the theme from

The Andy Griffith Show. Hermit, yes, easily,
  enclaved in disarray & neglected smells.

I've not seen where you live these days, in southeastern
  Georgia, with your girlfriend, four dogs,

three cats, an aggressive parrot named Hector
  whom she talks to in a high-pitched squeaky

voice, &, in a high-pitched squeaky voice,
  the parrot talks back. I dream you are happy

& at peace, tucked in, unbothered by those
    who would, easily, given the slightest

provocation, commit you to hospital or prison.
    Oh wary malcontent, recluse at ease when

your world is small enough to ignore, be safe.
    May you have, near at hand, whatever you need.

11

I saw the videoed newscasts,
newspaper articles, letters,
photographs, & you filled

in the blanks, of how, a year
after he & his wife found,
in their bed, on Christmas Eve,

their seventeen-year-old daughter
murdered, her boyfriend beside her,
a gunshot wound splattering

his brains across their wall,
his wife wrote a Dear-Santa letter—
a marketing ploy of a suburban

Cincinnati mall. She answered
the question, *Why does someone
you know deserve a special*

Christmas? To the facts of that
horror she added that her husband,
your first father, had *long ago,*

when he was still a teen,
had a son he'd lost track of.
A special Christmas for Dad

would be a reunion with
the boy. She won. The publicity
director swung into action

& that extended, romantic,
self-idealizing middle-American
family, Fundamentalists all,

wanted their lost lamb back;
never mind that *the teen father*
had abandoned his wife &

son; had threatened, &
attempted, to murder her;
had held the small boy to

the potty for hours, locking
him in the bathroom while
the child screamed & mother

cried & pounded, so determined
was he that a sixteen-month-old,
any boy of his, would no longer

shit in his pants. He hadn't cared,
then, what scars or terror
he'd instilled in the child,

but they knew nothing of this.
You were twenty-nine, a nursing
student, when Federal Express

arrived with a copy of the prize-
winning letter & tickets for
your Christmas Eve flight to

Covington, Kentucky. Journalists,
photographers, news teams
gathered, a ballooned festival

with commercially made
welcoming signs. You looked
exhausted, one hand up to shade

your face from the lights
as you came down the gangplank,
& what were you to do?—

Father & son step forward,
embrace sheepishly, step back
to behold one another, step

forward again & hug. Wild cheers.
Jingle Bells over the intercom.
Young man & old, same profile

& size, yes, you are his to share
with cousins, aunts, uncles,
stepmother, an entire panoply

of relations, mall-goers, newspaper
readers, the eleven o'clock news.
Then he steps to the mike & explains

how a youthful indiscretion is
being rectified this day, how he
had *lost touch with the mother*

who, subsequently, has gone on
to marry a number of times.
It is a circus act, & you,

dear one, roar at the lion tamer's
bidding—but, no, there is no
metaphor, no way to speak

of the claptrap Americans make
of the anguish they cannot live
with—especially if there's cash

to be made, as in this case,
end-of-the-year retail-season
profits. We blow our sorrows up,

record, broadcast, flood them
with light, corroding the dark
core with our voyeuristic

misfeasance. I'm raving, I know,
but there is Santa Claus standing
in the wings, & the manager

& publicity director of the mall
glowering over a wrong made right
through the generosity of its

corporate owners. The two of you
had nothing but half your genetic
code in common. It took less than

a week to disavow you of that
father, & the father who lost
a daughter, lost again his son.

12

Those few who might in this life come to know you,
read your novel perhaps, or your political essays,
even those who explore your website designed to sell
politically-biting & sexually explicit t-shirts,
bumperstickers, buttons, would think you eccentric.
Once you hawked them on a street in New York,
the thin, fold-away aluminum display table before you,
your dogs sleeping under the table, you in a navy
woolen cap pulled to mid-forehead, your torn
& dirty peacoat, the cold pulling up around you.
I watched you from a coffee shop across the street
& thought of those passing by who'd see you
as just another luckless vendor, a strange dude
down-&-out & loveless, but never as someone's
son, someone's boy beloved & worried about.
Yours is a brave & exhausting life, &, I suppose,
mine is too. And somehow we keep going, you & I,
doing the next thing, making of living, a life.
In the family we say, *he's quite a character, isn't he?*
then look away, our minds searching for a pattern
that might tell us what to make of you &
of ourselves with regard to you. You weren't
selling, started pacing & pounding your
gloved hands together, cupping them around
your mouth. So I went & got the van. You piled
the dogs in, your table, boxes, display boards.
On the way home, we talked about the war we
both opposed, the sorry state-of-affairs for those

without health care, for anyone disadvantaged,
anyone, or anyone's son or daughter. I felt, suddenly,
literally, it seemed, the weight of the world, as if
I were not just your mother, but cause of every
calamity our country had or ever would bring to bear
on its own unfortunates & those dwelling elsewhere.

yesterday driving back from Andover
south & west in the late February
mid-afternoon snow glare light I swung
off the interstate at Route 119

& headed into Groton past a grey
colonial you once rented a room in
then onto Chicopee Row past
the cemetery one-room schoolhouse

Gro-Lux metal works & up the drive
of the house we used to live in
the hemlocks I planted only inches
high now towering over the stone wall

you helped me—remember?—haul
the backfill no one home but I saw
again you pulling into the driveway
in your banana-yellow Chevrolet

or was it that white Nissan truck?
but this I am sure of the dogs ran
out & radio blaring you got out
& grabbed the collie by the front paws

danced with her the golden twirling
& barking you rocking your hips
kicking your feet & now the collie's
turn to bark-bark circle &

the golden's paws in your hands
doing the two-footed dog stomp
great commotion & I am happy
you're home watching from the window

over the kitchen sink evening sun setting
behind the pines & my quick turnaround
at the top of the drive we sold that house
fifteen years ago now & I see too

your wedding ceremony in our garden
when I glance over by the little Monet
bridge that spanned the fishpond
I filled in & planted with hollyhock

mallow lilies the lady justice of the peace
standing before you & Diane your
sister stepfather second father the bride
so sweet in a simple cotton dress

a small gold crucifix at her neck &
how did you look that June day? your
usual self-cropped haircut blue shirt tan
summer suit I was trying to make things

pleasant genial but neither of Diane's
parents came since they did not approve
her sister I think & a nephew &
niece a simple modest garden wedding

champagne cake & you two eager
to go toasted in an off-handed jokey
way the awkward blessing or wish
our family gets or gives as if no one

ever intends the changed state he or she
finds come to pass so let's make little
of it the kindest thing you ever said
about your wife was she is a keeper

but last time I saw her in Ukiah you
two separated she in a small apartment
regretted nothing she said except
that during her marriage she let your

atheism stop her from going to church
the light in the garden or restaurant
that evening in the trees behind the house
or on the hills over the roof the light

in the field at dawn or dusk the backdrop
that gives form to every shape but
nothing is remembered with enough
precision & no one is ever a keeper

14

It must have been February or early March 1962 when
     your grandfather drove me, his oldest,
across the Chesapeake Bay Bridge, through Annapolis
     & north to Baltimore. What your
grandmother thought best: I'd go away during this
     unpleasant business. Catholic Charities
would make sure I didn't catch a single glimpse of you,
     & you'd be a blessing for a childless,
deserving couple. A year from now—just think!—
     I'd be a typist somewhere, in D.C.
perhaps, no one the wiser, my future intact. Remnants
     of a snow were vanishing into
the salt marshes & stubble fields we passed, a cold,
     sunny afternoon. I wanted the
radio on, but Dad objected: *That's noise, not music.*
     We were silent, each of us
facing a prickly transition. When we found the home,
     on Crittenden Street, I told Dad
I'd go in alone. My act was unspeakable, its consequences
     to be borne with the least said,
but when my shaking hand froze on the car door's
     handle & I said, *I've seen all*
I need to see, let's go, he turned the ignition over.
     We just drove off.
I remember deliberately blurring my vision so I could
     dream more easily of love & romance
in an office setting, becoming an executive's wife,
     hosting dinner parties in a house

like those in the garden district we were passing through.
    A month later it was decided
I'd go to a home in Norfork, not Baltimore or Washington,
    further away, where I'd be less likely to—
who knows?—be spotted by a near-stranger
    who'd see my mother's daughter.

15

A few months before you were born, the American
        Red Cross sent a telegram on my behalf
to his C.O. in Düsseldorf, & your father got a three-
        week pass & a lift on a military cargo
plane so as not to embarrass the United States Army
        by adding another bastard to the citizenry.
Seventeen, just licensed, terrified of the rigs
        on the New Jersey Turnpike, I drove
all night to Fort Dix & somehow, in that maze
        of barracks & hangers, spotted him leaning
foot-up against a wall, cupping his hand to light a cigarette.

No way to tell you this except in spare terms: I had
        no context for what was happening
to my body or my mind. We drove to Elkton, Maryland,
        a place where anyone could
get married quickly, say on a Friday-night date.
        Billboards advertised cheap ceremonies.
No blood test, just proof you were at least sixteen
        & ten bucks. Bungalows both sides
for blocks along High Street, each a wedding
        chapel or a self-proclaimed church.
Because I liked the sound of its name, I chose
        the Alaskan Baptist Church of Our Lord
Jesus Christ Our Savior. A woman in a house dress
        let us in, her hair set in tight
bobby-pinned curls, a scarf pinned forward &
        then wrapped back & tied at the neck,

the way a woman often looked in those days
　　when you caught her at home.

I'll get him for you, she said. Two children in front
　　of a Philco TV. A short, hefty man
came out of a back bedroom & said, *So you want
　　to get married, huh?* waving his hand low
for us to stand in front of him, calling Ma back
　　from the kitchen to witness.
Then he held up a printed card & without
　　looking up read a short service.

I don't remember a ring. I stared at his wife's
　　tomato & flour-stained apron,
felt dizzy & hot, could see my box-cut tweed
　　jacket didn't hide my swollen belly.
Nothing corrodes like shame corrodes: an altar
　　becomes an apron, a prayerbook
becomes a card. Your tall, slope-shouldered
　　father　　wore his olive-green
Army dress uniform, held his visored cap
　　under his left arm, a gold braid
looped through the epaulette on his right shoulder
　　(close to my face as we stood),
a crossed-rifles sharpshooter badge over his
　　breast pocket. April 14, 1962,
almost a year to the day nearly twelve hundred
　　CIA-trained Cuban exiles were
captured in the Bay of Pigs; six weeks before
　　the Soviets offered Castro land-based
nuclear weapons. An interregnum of sorts.

On the TV, the Lone Ranger commanded Tonto
        who Kemosabe-d him: the sound
of horses galloping on hard dirt; *The William Tell*
        Overture. I'd refused to marry him

at first, my only moment of good sense, that's why
        this was so late an arrangement.
The push came to shove when your grandmother
        said I could not, unless married, come home,
& by then I wanted to keep my baby, keep you.

Perhaps I was stupefied or already dissociating.
        I had few words: . . . Say, *I will* . . .
Say, *I thee* . . . Thus your father & I stood in that
        hard-to-bear place & promised things
beyond us, yet not without joy. He was happy
        to drive around in our borrowed red
Corvair, to refer to you as *Little Scottie* knowing
        you'd be a boy, play baseball & football,
join the Army, bear the name he'd chosen. He wasn't
        yet shaving but was all swagger &
military lingo, glad to be stateside, to get a break
        from patrolling the border that divided Germany,
keeping the Commies out, keeping the Krauts in.

We drove to New York for a one-night honeymoon
        & found, at last, off Canal Street,
a cut-rate hotel, a small, dank room with one window
        open to an elevator shaft,
rose-&-trellis wallpaper tanned with age. Feeling
        woozy with humiliation & sick

with dread, I stared a long, long time at the interlocking
        stair-step pattern of the small black &
white tiles on that room's bathroom floor, not wanting
        to go to my soldier boy impatient on the bed.
I was hanging back from the bound-to-happen.

16

somewhere in the trickle or tumble of time 1971
I heard of Summerhill of A. S. Neill & Neill's
belief that *the function of a child is to live his
own life* so I walked around for days saying this
to you I wanted to stop stop stop shoving pills
down your throat or bribing you on a good day
sometimes child yes most days you on the floor
& me straddling you holding your nose if
I had to until you opened your mouth & you
kicking & screaming then zonked-out or not
up all night still wetting the bed at what seven
eight & suspended again for biting kicking
punching spitting more time in time-out than
time in class little boy blue so blue so blue so
red with fury or glum glum glum not a child living
his own life not a child functioning then I met these
hippies who were starting a free school—do you
remember Paul remember Sean David Helena?
first had to bring you down from three years
of ever-higher doses of Ritalin in a friend's
borrowed apartment just you & me locked in
& Carole King going on & on about there's
something wrong here there can be no denying
& three days & nights before you slept & I sat
or slept on the grey-green sofa in that shades-drawn
hot Takoma Park summer watching you hurl yourself
from wall to wall to floor to hall to bathroom to
kitchen to floor to bedroom to sofa to floor

an endless orbit of your three & a half-foot self
singing it's too late baby & thousands of fleas
in the orange shag rug & I feel the earth move
under my feet & we both scratched & bled you
mercilessly so I taped gloves over your hands & we
went for a drive while pest control smoked the place
with insecticide then back inside for a few more days
of sky tumblin' down & heart starts tremblin'.

17

enormous sycamores & ash lined
the streets of that 1920s neighbor-

hood we lived in when you were an ad-
olescent roots buckling the sidewalk

so it took caution to walk home modest
yards a bloomeria of lilacs azaleas dogwoods

an elementary school at one end &
a neighborhood market at the other

where you bagged groceries you &
your stepfather diametrically opposed

in all your manners-of-being you
physical loud imprecise irrational

he intellectual quiet accurate I don't think
either one of you had a stronger claim

on me but I felt defeated when I couldn't
broker—most of the time—a peace

between—you'd storm & bang doors
blast music worry from your basement

room he'd withdraw to bed curl into
a ball stay hidden & sullen for days

then there was the afternoon you cut off
your big toe with the lawnmower we rushed

you to the hospital the toe severed so
the best possible was to cover the wound

with a flap of your flesh you were weeks
in torment because some idiot of a doctor

realized you had an addictive personality
it was obvious even then at fourteen

so narcotics were withheld your
leg nerve firing off into the absent toe

gangrene setting in because you couldn't
keep still in pain so heal properly thus

I took up sewing to escape the silence &
the noise cut patterns & sat at my Singer

by an upstairs window stopping to look up
& out across backyards of willows maples

junipers scrub oak picturesque neighbor-
hood stitching going on inside the house

18

When I look back at the girl I was, she is as distant as a heron
    at the end of the marsh,
but each year the fog about her grows thinner & thinner—
    the fog of stupidity & prejudice—
& of the sorrow I feel for my mother who feared scorn,
    whose buried dreams
wracked her body, for my father's belief no decent man
    would ever have me. What were
the moonscape scratchings of that girl's nature that had
    her keep the child despite
each voice's admonition? How did she school herself into
    a generous life? I'd like to think
she saw a pattern beyond the evident confusion, but that
    wasn't so. She was lost & at risk,
probably delusional. Still she lived, the child I was who
    bore a child, as if she knew that if only
she'd grow light enough, there was someplace I'd finally
    carry her.

19

Do you remember a few years ago on Christmas Day
when your stepfather drove your second father's new
Mercedes coupe to Yarmouthport? You sat beside him

in your Jesus outfit & I was in the backseat, your
second father beside me staring blankly at the back
of your Jesus beard-&-hair combo wig. The car,

a gift for his boyfriend, a former Baltimore pimp
& heroin addict, had been, with your aid, stolen
back. Blind from AIDS-induced diabetes &

encephalopathy (because his anti-virals didn't cross
the blood-brain barrier but the virus had), he was losing
thousands of synaptical connections each day. His thin

carved-of-stone profile made him look like a shriven
Clint Eastwood. Because he couldn't see me, I felt free
to stare at him & wonder who once I was to have

loved him & carried our daughter & what strange
days & nights brought the four of us to that incongruous
journey . . . You were protesting the birth of Christ

& the suffering caused by religious doctrine.
The multi-colored striped bathrobe you wore,
tied around your middle with a yellow nylon rope,

I'd picked up years before at Goodwill. The crown
of thorns on your wig was a twig Christmas wreath.
You'd dabbed the tips with red nail polish. Stashed

in the trunk was the sign you carried around like
a doomsday character in a *New Yorker* cartoon.
It said, *Jesus is Make-Believe.* That summer you'd gone

out protesting when Fundamentalists gathered at those
stadium-sized revivals. So garbed, you wanted, above
all else, children to question God's existence. When

I wasn't looking at your second father, or at you, I kept
my eyes on the back of your stepfather's head, the thinned
hair separating around his scalp, his ponytail falling

to a silver S from his black cap. So large of mind
& heart, he has no considerations about my past,
about you. Your second father was estranged from

his boyfriend, thus staying with you, & thus the car
heist. He's a masochist, cold as a frost-bitten toad,
the boyfriend, a sadist. *Oh yeah, it's all S & M with*

them, you said yesterday, *whips, chains, cigarette*
burns up & down his spine. And they're into enemas
too, big time. I've seen the scars & hernias on his

abdomen. This was the tragedio-comedic, the ironically
absurd. Nothing to do but let the full force of it batter me
as it always has, as it always will. The day was cold,

overcast, a leveling sky, pearl-grey tinged from within
with peach. I remember glimpsing, between houses
on 6A, cloud-escaped spots of silvery light on the pewter

of Cape Cod Bay. How inviting those spots looked,
as if beckoning us to swim out that we might be
transported. Whence are we going? I wondered.

And whyfore? And witherest thou?

20

When you were at free school, finally off drugs,
a gifted teacher gave you a camera. When I miss
you most I pour over your photographs. The sycamore
leaves you caught as pale palms turned up &
floating on the skin of a brook—disembodied mercy
pleas adrift. Your self-portraits, body spread-eagled
& leaping from the top of a jungle-gym, or your face
atop a pillar in the June garden, whimsical or mischievous
as Pan. Because you bagged groceries at the market,
you've superimposed a close-up of your face over
the storefront, declaring the primacy of what was yours.
In your portraits of me I am always squinting—trying
to see the mercurial one behind the camera who has
escaped me, escaped from my body once, bloodied
& screaming, beginning this hurling apart of the twin
nebuli we were, gravity forcing more & more space
between us. I am pure space now when I wake at night
wanting you back inside me, wishing I'd wake to that
morning in the hospital when I was finally allowed
to unwrap you to see the sweet whole I'd made.
Perhaps that morning it was already too late, too late
for a girl who didn't want to be a mother, & the son
who couldn't stop running, for the man who says,
I'm changing, Mom, growing, & will say no more.

21

I had one night, two hours only, before the FCC threatened
    a lawsuit then shut you down,
to sit in a rented Corolla on a side street in Ukiah & listen
    to your voice broadcast
from the station you created. You built a transformer first,
    then taught yourself the craft.
Now you wrote & performed twelve hours a day, six days
    a week, programs that floated
from your small rented room—community, pirate radio,
    a six-mile radius—89.7 FM.

Your on-air voice sounded pleasant—you—but not quite.
    I could hear how your jaw
was clinched to tame your stutter & squeeze out this
    modulated deejay voice.
One of your shows was *The Atheists' Hour*—every Sunday
    morning to counter religious programming—
you'd begin with a weekly round-up of the imprisonments,
    torture & killings across the globe
committed in the name of one deity or another. At the end,
    you'd cackle & say, "The producer
of *The Atheists' Hour* wishes to thank . . . Satan!" You gave
    Friday nights, late, to *Skid Row,*
after scouring downtown for drunks & asking them
    to talk about their choice
to stay as intoxicated as possible for as long as possible.

During *The Grow-at-Home Companion* you conversed with those
    who enjoyed or required cannabis,

argued the pros & cons of various varietals & cultivation
      techniques. This was *Free Radio*,
&, on air, you were *The Captain* conducting a troupe
      of streetwise "associates" who'd come by
as scheduled or not, locals with names like Gruesome P.
      Jones, Trouthead, Ripe Cherry,
& Bong Brain—*tête-à-tête* buffoonery & barroom
      banter of a high, if salacious, order.

In one skit, you played Elvis & Devious Dave played
      Colonel Tom Parker—the two of you
quarreling & quipping rapid-fire over a proposed
      comeback from the grave—Presley
in an eternal hell of constipation, wanting to resurrect,
      but stuck on a toilet, loud farting
& worse, pared with riffs from *Love Me Tender* & *Hound
      Dog*.

With such high jinks & *high* compadres, your studio was
      subject to raids & wiretapping,
but you'd always wanted to stick it to authority, & now you
      had your means, your art.
By running fake ads & bogus public service
      announcements
      that spoofed bureaucratic absurdities
& legal legerdemains, you spoke for the oppressed &
      persecuted.

That night I let your voice lead me through the dizzying maze
      of your ingenious mind,
remembering the little boy who kept us in stitches. I admired
      your politics, your liberality,

your voice there on the fringe of the country, outrageous, brave,
   committed. Listening,
I no longer felt guilt toward you or shame for myself, only glad
   I'd kept you, that we were
in one another's life. And I saw then that you are mine & there
   is no mystery to it.

22

So this kid comes up & goes . . .

Hey, Mom, make a wish.
    I wish I could begin again with you.
    (Soft pale rust the color his hair's become).

So this kid comes up & goes . . . *Mom, make a wish.*
    I wish I were in a rocking chair & your
        infant head were pressed into my neck.

Mom, you're most like a zebra—calm & flashy.

So this kid comes up & goes . . . *Mom, make a wish.*
    I wish I were a pair of ragged claws . . .

No, Mom, be serious. Make a wish.

    I wish I'd never hit you or screamed at you.

Another wish, Mom. Please.
    I wish I'd always kept you close, had taken you with me.

      [So this kid comes up & makes us laugh,
         a natural joker. Kid jester.
            Kid clown. The kid cracks us up.
                Funny, funny kid—you can't help

      but smile, then he's got you, your poker face lost
        & he's happy,
            he's got you, made you laugh, made you cry,
                gotten to you . . .]

So this kid comes up & says, *Mom, Mom, it's me, your*
    own little boy. Says, *Mom,*

I'm not needed there any more.
Says, *Mom, this is too nice for me.*

Goes. The kid goes & dances with dogs, takes the two
toast-brown dogs & drives away in his white truck.
Billy & Milly.

Silly names for dogs. Silly means blessed, yes, blessed.

The kid comes up & goes . . . *Smile, Mom. It's not so bad.*
You'll see.

23

perhaps the son goes & one day comes back
or the sister goes & finds her brother &
his two dogs   brings them back
or the mother goes & finds her son &
the going back goes by way of compassion
for the self by the self   of sister for brother
of brother for sister   for the first & second
fathers & for the stepfather   [for fathers! for fathers!]
for the child who was who is not now a child
for the girl who was a mother [who is always a mother]
& the mother of the girl who is not & was
forgiveness like a cloth flying through the air
flying of its own accord billowing up & out
winds blowing across the cloth flying unanchored
& rippling with the screams of childbirth
screams that turn quiet   the quiet of the morning
after birth   of pale light in the room of first nursing
the cloth that flies through the air to bring
kindness to the child with his ardor to be born
& to the mother with her wish the child be parted
from her body   a song cloth sings to clouds
clouds tinted by time of day or night & the climate
the season   by the gritty or sheer quality of light
daughter unto mother unto grandmother unto son unto
father unto grandfather unto husband unto wife unto
corpse unto slippery-shouldered infant passing out
of the body   mothers turning toward daughters
toward sons & sons toward daughters forgiving

their mothers forgiving their fathers & nowhere
to be bourn on a cloth through the wind-rippled air
the cloth flying past this generation & the next
& the one unto that   the cloth shaded
or brightened by darkest night by brightest day
flying through windstorm & rainstorm
through blizzard & fog   unstoppable   unassailable
through drought & flood   flying light
wind-rippled cloth passing through air
& it is no more than this   no more than this

.

NOTES

#4 "the shapes/a bright container can contain" is from Theodore Roethke's poem "I Knew a Woman."

#17 I'm indebted to Mary Elizabeth Lang for discovering that "Kemosabe" means "faithful friend" or "trusty scout" and is a Potowatomie Indian word. *The Lone Ranger* originated at WXYX in Detroit, and one of the show's producers, Jim Jewell, had a father-in-law who ran a boy's camp in Michigan called "Camp Kee-mo-sah-bee." Thus this word made it into the living rooms of television viewers of the 1950s and 60s. From *The Lone Ranger*'s official website, devoted "to keeping the legend alive."

#22 "I wish I were a pair of ragged claws . . . " is from "The Love Song of J. Alfred Prufrock" by T. S. Eliot.

ACKNOWLEDGMENTS

The courage to write this memoir flew toward me when I read Richard Hoffman's essay "Backtalk: Notes Toward an Essay on the Memoir" (*http://www.abbington.com/ hoffman/memoir*). I am deeply grateful to Richard and to several other extraordinary writers who read this manuscript or portions thereof and who responded with encouragement and useful comments: Clare Rossini, Baron Wormser, Barbara Hurd, Carol Moldaw, Susan Morris, Janet Passehl, Susan Bouchard, Jeffrey Harrison, Elizabeth Garber, Robert Cording, Robert Dana, Shara McCallum, and Pit Pinegar. Each of the members of my remarkable poetry group, Brickwalk, did his or her critical best as I tinkered my way through early revisions: we are sixteen years together and counting, and I am deeply grateful to Jim and Susan Finnegan, Charlie Chase, Maria Sassi, Anne Sheffield, Clare Rossini, and Mary Elizabeth Lang (those active during the time I wrote this sequence). I am profoundly grateful to the Stonecoast MFA Program and to my students and teaching colleagues there, each a powerhouse who has swirled through my creative existence and nurtured me. My husband, Bruce Gregory, makes each generative moment possible: he is in many ways my source.

ABOUT THE AUTHOR

Gray Jacobik earned her Ph.D. in American and British literature from Brandeis University and for many years served as a professor of literature at Eastern Connecticut State University. She is a widely-published poet, recipient of a National Endowment for the Arts Fellowship in Creative Writing and an Artist's Fellowship from the Connecticut Commission on the Arts. Jacobik's work has appeared twice in *Best American Poetry* and in many other anthologies and journals including *Kenyon Review, Poetry, Ontario Review, Georgia Review, Connecticut Review,* and *Ploughshares.* She is winner of the Yeats Prize and the Emily Dickinson Prize and has received more than twenty nominations for a Pushcart Prize. In 2009 her poem "The Skeptic's Prayer" won the *Third Coast* Poetry Prize. Her book, *The Double Task,* University of Massachusetts Press, (1998), received the Juniper Prize and was nominated for the James Laughlin Award and the Poet's Prize. *The Surface of Last Scattering,* published by Texas Review Press (1999) was selected by X. J. Kennedy as the winner of the X. J. Kennedy Poetry Prize. *Brave Disguises* received the AWP Poetry Series Award for 2001 and was published by the University of Pittsburgh Press (2002). She served as the Robert Frost Poet-in-Residence at the Frost Place in the summer of 2002. From 2003 to 2009, she taught on the graduate faculty of the Stonecoast MFA Program. A painter as well as a poet, she lives in Deep River, Connecticut.

OTHER BOOKS IN
THE LAURELBOOKS SERIES

CAVANKERRY'S MISSION

Through publishing and programming, CavanKerry Press connects communities of writers with communities of readers. We publish poetry that reaches from the page to include the reader, by the finest new and established contemporary writers. Our programming brings our books and our poets to people where they live, cultivating new audiences and nourishing established ones.

CavanKerry now uses only recycled paper in its book production. Printing this book on 30% PCW and FSC certified paper saved 2 trees, 1 million BTUs of energy, 127 lbs. of CO_2, 67 lbs. of solid waste, and 524 gallons of water.